Conquering the
Book Thief

Carla Brown Shelton

ISBN 978-1-64559-989-0 (Paperback)
ISBN 978-1-64559-990-6 (Digital)

Covenant Books, Inc.
11661 Hwy 707
Murrells Inlet, SC 29576
www.covenantbooks.com

Acknowledgment

I want to acknowledge my husband for his patience and support. I am so thankful that God allowed you to come into my life. Forever grateful to you for your unconditional love.

I would also like to thank my Pastors, Bishop Owen and Pastor Tammy McManus for all your encouragement and support. You are spiritual jewels in the Kingdom of God.

In loving memory of my mom, Janice Mills Brown. You provided unconditional love and support despite limited resources. I am forever grateful for your contribution to my life. You instilled Christian values and showed me how to be a good mother. I watched you read the Word of God and saw how your life in Christ impacted so many people.

To my family, words cannot express how grateful I am for your love and support. Your encouragement has truly inspired me.

The thief comes only to steal and kill and destroy; I have come that they may have life and have it abundantly.

—John 10:10, KJV

Chapter 1
Missed Signal

They had a secret signal and could speak to each other without saying a word. This time Julia missed the secret signal and attempted to communicate with Nadia from across the room while Ms. Branch was doing a review for a math test. The girls were instructed to remain after class to discuss a consequence for their conduct in class. Nadia and Julia had been the best of friends since second grade. Nothing could separate the bond that these two sixth-grade girls shared. They were in the same class for the past four years. How could this be? The girls knew that this was just not a coincidence. Even though they shared the same classes, their backgrounds were far from similar.

Nadia was from a single-parent home. Her mother struggled to provide the basic necessities, but they were happy. Nadia rarely saw her father, but her mother provided a strong Christian home with sound biblical principles. Nadia's father disappeared when her mother became a Christian and began to live according to the Word of God. Nadia referred to her father as Dwight. She didn't think that he deserved to be called Dad because he had not fulfilled the role.

Nadia was not angry with her father. Her mother had expressed that they forgive him for not being a part of their lives. Nadia and her mother prayed for him often. They prayed that he would accept Jesus as his savior and that he would be happy. Nadia was happy in her humble abode. They rented a two-bedroom house on the other side of town. There wasn't room to play outside in the yard, but her mother made Nadia feel special and loved. Her mother would often tell Nadia that things would not always be this way. God would honor their faithfulness to him, and promotion was soon to come. When Nadia's mom spoke about promotion, she was referring to their financial status.

Julia's life was the exact opposite. Julia had both parents in the home, but they were not present in her life. Julia had the best of everything. She lived in a large two-story home and was also an only child. Julia often invited Nadia to her home for sleepovers. Julia loved the company of her best friend. Nadia was embarrassed to have Julia visit her home. Nadia's mom made sure that their home was neat and clean. However, it did not have all the amenities that Julia's parents could provide. Julia's parents were both corporate executives. They buried themselves in their work. Julia was only acknowledged when her performance in school was stellar. Julia knew that she was loved but felt that she had to work for their approval. Julia was encouraged to make good grades. Her parents stressed the importance of getting an education because it would be the gateway to success. Unlike Nadia, Julia's parents never mentioned anything about God. They made their charitable contributions to the local church, but they rarely attended. They felt that this was their duty to society because they had been so privileged. Julia's grandparents were so similar to her parents. They were stiff people and never really enjoyed meaningful relationships.

Julia felt a true connection with Nadia. Nadia was different. Nadia accepted Julia just because of who she was and not because of what she possessed. They had become the best of friends. They enjoyed watching Nickelodeon. They laughed about the same corny jokes. They liked similar foods and played some of the same games. They were like sisters. Nadia and Julia never looked at the color of their skin. All they knew was that they enjoyed each other's company.

Neither girl looked forward to the punishment that awaited them. Ms. Branch was a strict teacher, and her instructional time was valuable. She maintained order in her classroom, and distractions were few. Ms. Branch knew the relationship between the two girls, but she wasn't sure why they choose to disrupt her lesson. Nadia and Julia never got into trouble. They were good students. Ms. Branch normally called parents about any issue that occurred in her class. Nadia did not want her mom to be contacted about such a minor incident. Julia only received positive phone calls home, and this would be out of the ordinary. Both girls begged Ms. Branch not to call their parents, and they promised that this would never happen again. Ms. Branch accepted their apology, and they served a lunch detention because of their conduct in class. They ate their lunch in silence while Ms. Branch graded papers and checked her email.

After lunch detention, Julia wanted to know what was so important that she needed to tell her. Nadia said, "I need your help with this lesson." Julia was a bright student. She had a private tutor that assisted her in the afternoon. Nadia was a bright girl, but she had to work hard to maintain her grades. Julia did not have to work as hard. The classwork was easy for her, but the tutor provided additional support. Julia was glad to help her friend. So many other friends had betrayed Julia in the past. Nadia was the only person that remained loyal to her after all these years.

Days had passed and both girls were elated to learn that Ms. Branch had kept her promise. She did not contact their parents. Things would be different. No more missed signals and no more lunch detentions. The weekend was approaching, and the plans were already underway. Julia had plans to attend the movies and visit the zoo. Of course, Nadia would be her invited guest to attend these events.

Chapter 2
A Secret Revealed

Months had passed since the incident with Ms. Branch, and it was obvious that Julia was different. Nadia prodded her for answers, and each time it was the same. Nothing is wrong. Nadia couldn't figure this out. "We got caught disrupting the class, and we served a lunch detention. Our parents were not contacted." Both girls were relieved, but Julia appeared distant.

They still laughed at the same corny jokes and participated in the same events, but something was different. Nadia knew that she hadn't betrayed the trust of her dear friend. What could be wrong?

Nadia was so disturbed by her friend's actions that she shared it with her mom. Nadia knew what her mom's response would be: "Let's pray." This was her answer for everything. So that's exactly what they did. They began to ask God to help her dear friend.

Each year in October, their middle school hosted a bookfair. The school would advertise the event, and kids would be encouraged to bring money to buy books and all sorts of other trinkets that were for sale. Nadia knew that their funds were limited in her household, so she never made a big deal about purchasing items at the bookfair.

The kids were always allowed to preview the items on the Friday before the actual event was scheduled to begin. Nadia loved to read, but one of her favorite things was the scented erasers. She had saved a couple of dollars but wanted to buy something for her mom at Christmas. Nadia's mom worked hard to provide for her basic needs.

Nadia made the decision to give her mom something at Christmas and not waste it on scented erasers. Her mom was more precious to her than the scented erasers.

On the other hand, Julia had preselected several books and other items that she wanted to purchase. There was excitement in the air as the children went into the library to make their purchases. As the students boarded the bus at dismissal time, Julia raced to catch up with Nadia. She showed Nadia all of her purchases with excitement in her eyes. Julia got close to her friend as Nadia walked to board the bus.

Julia told Nadia, "I've got something to tell you. Call me when you get home?"

Nadia boarded the bus as Julia was a car rider. Nadia couldn't help but wonder what the secret was. Why was Julia so excited? She noticed a big difference in her friend. There seemed to be a noticeable difference in Julia today as in previous months. What could be the result of this sudden change in her friend?

As Nadia arrived home from school, she raced to the kitchen to get a snack. She called her mom at work to let her know that she had arrived. Nadia lived next door to an elderly neighbor named Ms. Simmons. Ms. Simmons would watch out for Nadia until her mom arrived. Next, she would get a snack and relax in front of the TV before beginning her homework assignments. This was her normal routine. However, she remembered the conversation that she had had with Julia at dismissal time. Nadia knew that Julia would be accompanied by her tutor. She still gave Julia a call and asked her to call her back once she was free to speak in private.

Around thirty minutes later, Nadia received a call from Julia. Julia beamed with excitement. She was gasping for air as she described what she had purchased at the bookfair. Nadia thought that this was nothing unusual. Julia always purchased an array of items at the bookfair, including books, pencils, erasers, and bookmarkers. What was so different this time? Julia exclaimed that she had the money to purchase all the things that she had preselected, but this time she took a book and some other items without paying, and no one noticed a thing.

Nadia gasped on the other end of the phone. She couldn't believe what she had just heard. Her dear friend had done the unspeakable. She took items from the bookfair without paying for them, and she was absolutely elated about her adventure.

Julia explained that she was able to keep the money that her parents had given her. Why? What was going through her mind as she was committing this crime and such a sinful act? She continued to talk about her exploit as Nadia sat in utter silence. Nadia was speechless. She didn't know what to say as Julia revealed this secret to her best friend. Julia asked Nadia not to mention this information to anyone. Of course, Nadia agreed because this was her best friend. Nadia felt an uneasiness in her stomach, and she couldn't believe her ears. Who was this person on the other end of the phone? This was not the Julia that she had known for the past four years. Nadia's only response to this situation was *Why*? Julia had the money to purchase whatever she wanted, and she chose to steal from the school's bookfair!

The profit from the sales were used to purchase other books and supplies for their school. Julia exclaimed that it was only a couple of dollars and no one would miss a couple of dollars. What was the big deal? This was a big deal to Nadia. Nadia's mom had instilled Christian values in her, and she could not ignore the fact that this was a sin. Julia had violated one of the Ten Commandments, and she had no remorse, and this meant nothing to her.

Nadia told Julia that she had to go get started on her homework and they would talk later. Julia stressed that this was a big secret between them, and no one should know about this. Nadia swore to secrecy and proceeded to get started with her homework. However, she was so distracted by the conversation that had just transpired. Who is this girl named Julia? Nadia never dreamed that her best friend would steal items, especially from their school's bookfair.

Even though the items were small and insignificant, it was the principle. As the days went by, they still did not discuss the incident. However, Julia maintained that this was a one-time event and it would never happen again. Nadia felt a little better after hearing her best friend say that it had only happened once and that it wouldn't happen again. Nadia was relieved to hear this. She wanted to believe her friend. Anyway, we all make mistakes, and we learn from them. This is the motto that Nadia's mom firmly supports. Nadia was a trustworthy friend. She kept this secret in strict confidence.

However, things were different between the two girls. Their relationship was different, and Julia could sense the tension between them. No one else saw the girls any other way but merely best buds.

The fall leaves covered the ground, and Thanksgiving was right around the corner. Parent/teacher conferences were being held, and the parents had an opportunity to visit with teachers and get updates on grades and behavior. Julia's mom made it a point to put this on her calendar at work. She loved hearing all the wonderful comments about her daughter's academic performance and her behavior.

Julia had taken an interest in the band and wanted to play the clarinet. Julia's mom met with the band director to discuss the instrument selection and the obligations that would be required for her participation.

Nadia's mom was equally interested in her daughter's academic performance and behavior. However, she wasn't as fortunate to get off work to come meet with teachers. She mainly communicated with them via email or phone. Nadia's mom needed the hours at work and couldn't afford to take the deduction. She was a department manager at Walmart, and any time away from the store, the hours would be deducted from her paycheck. She needed to work, and Nadia understood.

Nadia had taken an interest in the school choir. Nadia wanted to participate in the band but didn't want to stress her mom with the added cost of the instrument rental fee, so she chose to participate in the school choir. There was no cost associated with singing in the choir. Nadia already had the items that were required for performances in her closet at home. This included a black skirt and a white blouse.

The girls still remained good friends even though their interests were separating them. They were beginning to develop other friendships, and there was very little supervision required because Nadia was well-behaved just like Julia. Julia's mom didn't mind paying the expenses for the weekend sleepovers. These sleepovers allowed Julia's mom the opportunity to catch up on work obligations and emails while Julia was occupied with her best friend. Julia's dad entertained himself with repairing an antique car that was stored in the spare garage. This allowed him the opportunity to unwind and relieve stress. With both parents being occupied with their own agendas, there was little time for Julia. Julia 's entertainment was Nadia. Julia was missing something, but she found it hard to express this as a sixth grader. She was intelligent and excelled academically but couldn't really reflect on what she was feeling. Julia knew that something was missing.

Chapter 3
Christmas Is Here!

Fall quickly faded into winter. Shortly after Thanksgiving vacation, Christmas was right around the corner. Nadia's mom tried to get as many hours at work as possible. She wanted to provide a wonderful Christmas experience for her daughter, but she knew that nothing could replace the special time that they spent together. Nadia's mom reluctantly took advantage of the sleepovers at Julia's house. She took advantage of that time so that she could earn extra money.

Nadia and her mom decorated their Christmas tree on the first Saturday in December. That was their family tradition. Nadia's mom had Christmas music playing loudly in the background as they decorated the tree together. Nadia enjoyed this more than anything. Her mom made her feel special and loved even though they had limited finances. They would sing to the music and laugh as they were often off-key. This is why Nadia chose to sing in the choir at school. It reminded her of the joy that she experienced with her mom. Nadia was happy being with her mom, but she longed to have a dad.

Nadia's dad would come over to visit on Christmas Day every year, but it was such an awkward experience. Nadia's dad seemed like a stranger. He didn't know her, and she didn't know him. He asked the same questions each time they saw each other, and the answer was always the same. He wanted to know how she was doing in school, and the answer was always "Good." Nadia could tell that there was a sadness on his face. He seemed empty, and her mom would always say that he needed Jesus. Nadia's mom never spoke of him in a negative way but wished him well. Nadia wanted to make him a part of her life. She could feel his sadness, and she could see it in his eyes. Nadia had written letters to her dad and kept them in a secret journal hidden in her room. She told him how much she missed having him in her life and hoped that one day that they could have a meaningful relationship. Nadia often wondered if she were a boy, if things would be different between her and her dad.

Christmas Day arrived, and it looked different in both households. Julia's family had an elaborate tree, and they took family photos in front of the tree each year. They would send these photos out as greeting cards to family and friends. Julia would wake up early and race downstairs to see what was under the tree. Her mom would take photos of Julia opening up her gifts and post them on Facebook. Christmas Day was a time when Julia felt like she had a real family. There was laughter and excitement that filled the room as they opened their gifts. Breakfast followed, and Julia continued to play with her new toys as the day progressed. Her grandparents would come over and eat Christmas dinner with them. They ate at the dining room table. It was elegantly decorated this time of year. They only ate at the dining table during Thanksgiving and Christmas. They would bring out the baby photos and reminisce about earlier times. The conversation would fade to work and work issues. Julia associated these times with happiness even though it may be short-lived.

Nadia would wake up and run to the Christmas tree. She wasn't allowed to open up any gifts until they did their family tradition. Each year they would purchase birthday balloons. They would release them in the air and sing "Happy birthday" to Jesus before any gifts could be opened. Nadia looked forward to going to Dollar Tree each year and picking out the balloons. This was a special time for her and her mom. They were happy despite their circumstances. Nadia would get one gift that she really wanted, and the other gifts were clothes and games. She knew that this was all her mom could afford. Dwight, Nadia's dad, would come over to wish them a merry Christmas, and he would give her mom a little envelope with money inside. It wasn't much, but they were grateful. Nadia wanted to feel like a family, but it was all so awkward. Dwight would stay for about an hour, and then he would wander off to his mom's house where he lived. He had lived with them for years before Nadia was born. When Nadia turned two years old, her mom decided that he couldn't continue to stay with them because they weren't married. She accepted Jesus as her personal Savior, and she was completely sold out to her new faith and refused to compromise. Nadia knew that Dwight still loved her mom, but he was unable to fulfill the new requirements that she demanded. Nadia's mom would say that sin is comfortable for a season. Nadia didn't know what she was talking about but listened and nodded politely. Sometimes Nadia felt that her newfound relationship with Jesus replaced Dwight. Essentially, it did. This had been the routine for Nadia for the past four years. After opening gifts, they would enjoy a big breakfast and then lie on the couch and sleep for a while.

The cooking began, and they would travel to an aunt's house and continue the celebration. It was loud, and kids were everywhere. It was just right for her. The kids would eat Christmas dinner first, and then the adults would eat last. It was nothing fancy, but laughter was in the air. This was the best time ever.

The only thing that Nadia didn't like about Christmas was that when it ended, her mom would have to return back to work and deal with all those store returns. It was exhausting for her mom, and Nadia spent the remainder of the Christmas break with her aunt and cousins. Nadia loved her aunt, but the routines were so different at her aunt's house. Essentially, there were none. It was basically chaos all the time. Nadia loved her aunt but missed the structured environment that she had at home.

Nadia and Julia reconnected over the Christmas break, and they were able to spend some time together, but it wasn't much. Julia had structure at her house. There was a schedule on the bulletin board in the kitchen that Julia reviewed daily to know about the activities that were planned for that particular day.

They had the opportunity to attend the movies and exchange Christmas details. Nadia noticed that Julia was different. Julia was still distant even though she enjoyed the time that they spent together.

Not a Happy New Year

Everyone was sad about returning back to school. The kids were tired as they entered the door. However, this was the case on the first day back after a long holiday break. Children were dressed in new coats and sneakers that they had received as Christmas presents. The students were excited about beginning the new year because it meant that half of the year was over and they were on a short stretch to the end of the school year. Children shared stories with their teachers and friends about their Christmas break experience.

Shortly after arrival to school, Julia was called to the office. This was very unusual. She wondered if her mom had made different plans for her after school. The school secretary asked Julia to wait in the office. Julia was definitely puzzled. What was this all about? The principal beckoned for Julia to come into his office. When she came into the office, he appeared distraught. This made Julia nervous. Julia had never been in trouble. She was a model student and well-liked by her peers and teachers. The principal began to share that over the break they had come into the building to work on repairs in the library and other parts of the school. They reviewed some of the surveillance video from the library and noticed that Julia had taken books and other items from the bookfair. Julia was disappointed. She thought that this had gone unnoticed. She believed that she was home free with the items that she had taken. She had really forgotten all about the bookfair. The principal and assistant principal reviewed the video surveillance and shared with her that she had been caught taking things from the bookfair without paying. Julia was not able to view everything from the camera footage because of confidentiality.

Mr. Wiley, the principal, explained that this was an investigation that had taken place over the break and they didn't want to share information with parents until their findings were complete. Julia was asked to write a statement about what happened on that day. In her statement, she admitted that she had taken the items without paying. There was no reason to lie because of the evidence on the videotape. Mr. Wiley explained to Julia that her parents would be contacted, and disciplinary actions would be taken because of the severity of the incident. Julia was speechless. She thought that since so much time had passed since the bookfair, she had gotten away with the crime. What would her parents think?

Julia remained in the office for the first part of the school day. Her parents were contacted and were asked to come to the school to address the issue. Julia was so nervous about the fact that both her parents were being asked to leave their jobs and come to the school. Julia knew how important their professions were to her parents. As Julia waited for the arrival of her parents, her heart sank in her chest. What would they think of her? Image was everything to her parents.

When her parents finally arrived, they were clearly upset and looked distraught as well. Surely, there must have been a mistake made, and they were willing to forgive the whole matter. Unfortunately, it was not a mistake. Mr. Wiley explained to the parents that the surveillance camera clearly showed that Julia was observed taking books and other items from the bookfair and walking away without paying. The parents insisted on seeing the tape, but because of confidentiality, they were not allowed to see the other children. Mr. Wiley assured the parents that it was indeed Julia in the video that they had observed. In addition to this, Julia admitted to taking the items without paying. Well, Julia's parents had no recourse but to submit to the evidence and take the consequence that was issued. Julia was suspended for three days and was asked to pay restitution for the items. She was also instructed to meet with the school counselor to discuss the issue. The parents agreed with everything that was asked of them. They were also asked to take Julia home for the remainder of the day. This would serve as day one of the suspension.

As they got into the car, her parents were concerned about leaving work and their public image. They made phone calls to their jobs about an issue at school and how they would be returning as soon as arrangements were made to accommodate Julia for the next two days. Her parents simply said that they were disappointed and told her that she was punished for the next two weeks. They failed to ask her what she had taken and why. They were so preoccupied with their own lives that they continued to neglect her. Julia felt confused. This was not at all what she expected. Her parents simply brushed the whole incident under the rug. Julia was disappointed. She felt as if she wanted her parents to be upset with her. They explained to her that this was such a childish incident and they couldn't understand why something like this happened. But they insisted that this would *never* happen again. For some strange reason, Julia wanted more severe consequences from her parents. If she were punished severely, then it would make her feel as if they cared.

Julia's parents made arrangements for her to remain with her grandparents for the duration of the suspension. She was also surprised at her grandparents' reaction as well. They remained cold and stoic. They shared that they were disappointed in her behavior and insisted that no one in their family had ever done such a thing. She was scolded for a few minutes, and that was the end of the conversation.

For the next three days, Nadia didn't know what had happened to her friend. Because Julia was punished, she was unable to connect with her friend. The time away from school made Julia feel more distant than ever. Julia felt lonely and also angry, but she didn't know why. After returning back to school, she explained everything to Nadia. At least Nadia was glad that the secret was out in the open, and she hoped that it would never happen again.

Chapter 4
Meeting with the School Counselor

After Julia was caught stealing from the bookfair, the principal suggested that Julia see the school counselor. Her parents were not excited about the idea but chose to accept the advice of the principal. Julia's parents were so embarrassed about their daughter's behavior, and they wanted to keep their public image squeaky clean.

Ms. Daniels was the school counselor. She was a middle-aged African American female who genuinely cared about children. She wanted all children to be successful no matter what barriers existed in their personal lives. She had a true passion about her job. She had worked as a school counselor for twenty years and was eager to work with Julia. Ms. Daniels was a Christian. She actually displayed the title in everything that she did. Teachers would often come to her for advice, and she would always find a way to squeeze in the name of Jesus into her conversations. Ms. Daniels knew that she was not allowed to share her faith with the students, but she would always pray before each counseling session so that the therapy would be successful, and students would leave transformed. Ms. Daniels loved the Word of God. She would spend her spare time researching the Bible and preparing for her weekly Bible study lessons. She held Bible study in her home and enjoyed the fellowship with other believers and expounding on the Word of God. Ms. Daniels would invite the teachers at her school to attend her Bible study, but no one took her up on the offer. Several teachers expressed an interest, and that's as far as it went.

Ms. Daniels welcomed Julia into her office and explained about the rules of confidentiality. Ms. Daniels sensed that Julia was nervous and didn't know what to expect. Ms. Daniels and Julia played some games to ease the tension. She noticed that the atmosphere in the room was changing. It was obvious that Julia was getting a little more relaxed and this counseling thing was not as bad as she had expected.

The time went by fast, and before she knew it, Julia had to return to her next class. Julia had never actually known what Ms. Daniels's job entailed. Ms. Daniels went into the classroom and taught lessons about careers, study skills, and getting along with peers, etc. Julia didn't know that Ms. Daniels actually worked with students privately. This was never a need that Julia had until she was discovered taking things from the library. Ms. Daniels was so patient with Julia. She helped Julia to take a journey of true discovery and self-realization. Ms. Daniels helped Julia to understand that her real issue was not stealing from the bookstore.

Julia was actually excited to visit the school counselor each week. Julia didn't mention to Nadia that she was seeing Ms. Daniels because she wanted to keep everything private as she was instructed. The next few weeks were difficult for Julia. She and Ms. Daniels talked about some difficult issues regarding her family. Ms. Daniels helped Julia to realize some feelings that she had never discussed. It was just a product of the pain that she was feeling. Julia had buried her pain so deep inside that she had become numb. Julia wanted the love and acceptance from her parents. Even though Julia had two parents in the home, they were absent in her life. Ms. Daniels helped Julia to forgive her parents for their behavior toward her. Julia felt rejected and unloved by her parents. They rarely spent time with her. Ms. Daniels shared that time equals love. Julia also learned that this is the same way that her parents had been treated by her grandparents. This was a vicious cycle that was repeating itself. Julia never looked at her

CONQUERING THE BOOK THIEF

situation like this before and was able to see it clearly through new lenses.

The school counselor helped Julia to realize that she was performing for the approval of her parents and not for the fulfillment of herself. Julia was seeking the approval of her parents' love by her academic performance which had left her empty and lonely. She needed to find fulfillment in herself. Julia understood that her emptiness was created by her own inadequacies. She longed to be loved by her parents, and the only way that she felt a glimpse of that love was through her achievement in school. Her parents experienced that same longing and need for approval. They felt that if they achieved success on their jobs, then they would have value and acceptance. They had imparted this same level of expectation onto their daughter. It was what they had both learned from their parents. How could this be wrong? This is what they had come to know as children and had raised their daughter with the same unrealistic expectations.

Julia had learned through counseling that the void that she longed to fill was that of love. She needed to be loved and accepted for who she was and not for what she was able to accomplish. Stealing the book was only a by-product of the pain that she was experiencing as a child and not as a daughter. Her parents were not really able to comprehend what was going on in their daughter's mind but only knew that they wanted the best for her. They were achievers who performed for the approval of others and wanted to be accepted into society by their associates. However, this had left them lonely and dejected when they were unable to comply with the social demands of society.

The Best Weekend Ever

After several weeks of therapy, Julia decided that she wanted to spend the weekend with Nadia. Nadia was shocked. Nadia asked her mom's permission, and they graciously agreed to accept this guest into their home. It was a normal weekend with just movies and board games. Julia had wished that this

21

would have happened earlier. They enjoyed being together like old times. On Sunday, Nadia's mom expected everyone to attend church. Julia was never a regular church attender. Julia's family attended church on Easter, Mother's Day, and New Year's. Julia was kind of nervous about what to expect. First of all, this was a predominantly African American church service. Julia always felt comfortable around Nadia and her mom, but what about a whole congregation of people that she didn't know? Nadia's mom prepared sausage, grits, and eggs for breakfast. They giggled at the table while they ate their food. Julia felt butterflies in her stomach because this was something so unusual to her. She didn't know what to expect. Both girls got dressed for church in casual attire. They arrived for church around 8:45 a.m. as the service was scheduled to begin at 9:00 a.m. As they entered the church, they were greeted by people standing at the door. They embraced Julia with such a warmth that she had never experienced before in her life. She was given a visitor badge with her name on it. She was instructed to stand when first-time visitors were recognized. Julia noticed that the church was filled with all type of people. It was not just an African American church, but there were Hispanics, white people, and everybody seemed so happy. This was definitely different, but Julia liked what she saw so far. As they entered the sanctuary, it was dark inside. The lights were on the stage, and then Nadia's mom sat very close to the front of the sanctuary.

As the clock on the wall struck promptly 9:00 a.m., the praise team began to sing songs of praise to the Lord. Julia didn't know any of the songs, but the words were displayed on this huge screen. Nadia's mom ran to the front of the church and began to kneel as the songs penetrated her heart. The lead praise singer belted out the worship songs as if Jesus Himself was standing right in front of her. Nadia closed her eyes and raised her hands as well. Julia looked around the sanctuary, and there were other children and adults who were in the same posture. Julia was in awe until the praise team sang one song that seemed to touch her in a special way. Julia began to weep, and she didn't know why. She couldn't explain what was happening. She wasn't in pain nor was she afraid. Julia felt something inside her that she had never felt before, and she wasn't able to explain it in her head what was taking place at this very moment. All she knew was that she wanted to remain in this atmosphere. It felt warm, and she was comfortable even though the only people that she knew were Nadia and her mom. It felt like the joy she felt on Christmas morning but a hundred times greater.

After the worship ended, the people returned back to their seats, but Julia was still in awe. She liked the music and didn't want the sounds to end. Next, the pastor's wife got up and welcomed the first-time guests. Julia felt a flood of love from strangers that she had never met. They made her feel wanted and most importantly, welcomed.

Who are these people? Did any of them know my parents? So many questions ran through Julia's mind. Nadia sat next to her and smiled. Nadia was so glad that her best friend was finally able to experience her Jesus and her lifestyle. This is the life that Nadia loved and embraced. Not because her mom loved the Lord, but because he had become real to Nadia as well. Nadia watched as her friend was being introduced to the person and presence of Jesus. Julia was speechless. Julia just observed everything that was taking place.

The pastor came up and preached a sermon that was easy to understand even to a sixth grader. Julia hung onto his every word. Not only that; he didn't look like a pastor. He was a handsome man that was casually dressed and was very easy to understand. After the sermon, the pastor prayed for people and asked if anyone wanted to receive Jesus as their Lord and Savior. Julia didn't know how she managed to be in the line after the invitation was made. How did I get here? She felt drawn to the altar. No one encouraged her to go up, but she found herself in the line next to other people who wanted to receive Jesus as their Lord and Savior.

Nadia watched as her friend accepted Jesus as her Lord and Savior. Tears filled Nadia's eyes. Nadia and her mom had prayed for Julia to receive the Lord as her personal savior for such a long time. This was answered prayer that stood right in front of them.

After the service, Julia reconnected with Nadia and her mom. There was such excitement in Nadia's eyes, and she couldn't wait to hear about her friend's experience. Julia got into the car and was lost for words. She couldn't begin to describe what had just transpired. Nadia's mom described it best when she said transformation.

In Julia's eyes, everything was different. Nothing appeared to be the same. What happened to her was amazing, and she couldn't describe it. All she knew was she wasn't the same. As they arrived back to Nadia's house, they ate lunch, and Julia packed her things and was transported back to her home. Even though the weekend was relatively inexpensive and simple, it was the best time of her life. Julia felt complete. She felt whole, and her life had meaning. She knew that this was unusual for a sixth grader, but it was real, and she wanted to share this experience with her parents. Nadia's mom dropped Julia off at her home. Julia wasn't ready to go home. She wanted to remain with her best friend and her mom in their environment. Nadia's home lacked in appearance, and the amenities that Julia was accustomed to, but there was such a calmness and peace there that Julia enjoyed.

Chapter 5
Spring Break

As the weeks passed, Julia and Nadia shared an even deeper connection than before. Julia often wondered why she had never spent the weekend with Nadia until now. They both realized that the timing just wasn't right until now.

Nadia's mom welcomed Julia to come back and visit them on the weekends whenever she was off from her job. They spent more time together, and they even began to pray together. Julia felt a real connection with her newfound relationship with Jesus and this family. Julia would share this experience with her family, and sometimes they seemed uninterested. Other times, they began to listen and wonder what had happened to their daughter. She seemed different. Julia smiled more and had such a joy that showed on her face. Julia would talk with her parents about Nadia's church and encouraged them to join her in a church service. Julia would go on and on about every little detail of the church service, and there was such excitement in her voice when she spoke of the church experience. This was all she seemed to talk about lately.

As spring break was approaching, Julia begged her parents to join her in a service at Nadia's church. This seemed so important to Julia. Julia's parents wanted to continue with their Easter tradition at their church, but Julia was adamant about attending the service at this new church. Julia finally convinced her parents to attend Easter service at the new church. Julia's parents were welcomed at the door by a huge embrace. Julia's parents didn't know what to expect next. As they entered the sanctuary, things were a lot different from what they were accustomed to at their church when they attended, which was not often. The praise team began to sing worship songs, and Julia pointed to the screen on the wall so that they could follow along. The service was phenomenal. The church did a reenactment of the resurrection of Jesus. It was so moving. There was not a dry eye in the church. Julia was waiting to see if her parents would go to the altar to accept Jesus, but they didn't. Julia knew that they were impacted by the performance but didn't give up hope that they would experience the same transformation that took place in her own life.

How could a little rich girl who was once considered a book thief now be transformed to follow Jesus? This is the reality of how our lives can be transformed in an instant. Julia was not disappointed that her parents did not go up to the altar, but she was convinced that something happened to them. This was just a seed that had been planted, and it needed to be nurtured in order to grow. Julia learned of the forgiveness of Jesus and had forgiven herself and her parents. The unrealistic expectations were a thing of the past. Julia had learned from Nadia how to accept people right where they are and not for what they can do for you. That's what Julia and Nadia's relationship had been built upon. No expectations. This is how Jesus accepts us. There are no expectations. He loves us right where we are.

Julia's transformation was evident to everyone around her. Her parents noticed a change in their daughter. Julia loved the atmosphere at Nadia's church but wasn't able to visit as often as she'd liked. Nadia's mom worked on some Sundays, so the sleepovers were not always possible. However, Julia would ask her parents to bring her to church. They would oblige their daughter when their workload was not overwhelming. Julia's parents spent Sunday mornings catching up on work and preparing for the upcoming week. Julia's dad would work on his car in the garage away from everyone.

Julia had learned how to pray for her parents' salvation. Although Julia didn't see a change in her parents, she had changed her feelings toward them. Julia was no longer empty inside, and the void that she had experienced was now replaced with the love of Jesus. Julia's transformation made a huge impact on her. She no longer lived for the approval of her parents but made strides to help others that she connected with on a day-to-day basis. Julia felt such a freedom because she had truly forgiven her parents. Julia and Nadia were inseparable, but now Julia was more outgoing and shared her joy with everyone around her. Julia felt like she wanted others to feel the same freedom that she experienced.

Even though this is a fictional story about the transformation of one little girl, this too can be your story. Do you have wounds from the past? Has your relationship with your parents been stellar? Most of our childhood experiences have left us damaged or wounded from some or many incidents. We all long to have the perfect relationship with our parents. Maybe that was not the case. What if our parents were not present, or what if they disappointed us in some way? At some point, they didn't give us everything that we needed. Only the love from our heavenly Father can erase the pain from our past and make us brand-new.

We live in an imperfect world. We tend to keep score for how we have been wronged by people that we encounter. We can remember vividly what someone said to us that offended us. We fail to recall the good times. The enemy makes it a point to remind of us what took place each time we run into that person or someone mentions their name. We even become so clever as to hide whenever we see them because we don't want to relive that painful event. Sometimes the other person is completely unaware of the pain that they have caused, but we can't seem to forget. This is called an offense. Jesus speaks of offenses in Luke 17:1. He said to his disciples that it is impossible, but that offenses will come, but woe unto him, through whom they come.

Chapter 6
Rejection and Abandonment

What does rejection actually mean? It is the actual act of not feeling wanted or welcomed. Let me give you a modern-day example of rejection. Everyone in your office may have been invited to a party, but you did not receive an invitation. The enemy suddenly comes into this situation and causes mental distress. He begins to plant thoughts in your head that nobody wants to be around you. You are not welcomed. You begin to feel uneasy around the person who is giving the party, and thus feelings of rejection, coupled with offense, have set inside your heart. You tell yourself that you didn't want to go to this party anyway when in fact, you were excited when others shared the news that this event would be taking place.

We use these excuses as defense mechanisms to make us feel better about not being included. This is just a small example of rejection, but how does this apply to a child? Let me share how rejection and abandonment go hand in hand. Perhaps your father was absent from the home for whatever reason. You were left at home in the care of your mother, and she rarely discussed the issues surrounding his absence. Thus, you are left to formulate your own ideas of why your father was not present. You begin to formulate ideas in your mind as to why he is not a part of your life. You even blame your own birth for his leaving. The enemy has used this lack of communication with your mother about this situation. The enemy has planted seeds of doubt inside your mind that you were the reason that he left the home. Then the enemy moves on a little bit further and tells you that you were a mistake and that your dad didn't want a child at the time. This may *all* be a lie, but you tend to believe this lie because you have no other information to support his absence. Thus, you have bitten the bait, and now the enemy will flood your mind with all types of lies, and then your heart is affected. Consequently, rejection and abandonment have entered your heart and mind. So many people have faced rejection at some point in our lives as a child. We tend to grow up with these unresolved emotional wounds. If the wound of rejection and abandonment is not healed and cleansed from our heart, it grows into even bigger issues, such as trust, jealousy, intimidation, self-pity, shame, and even rebellion.

My own father was not present in my life. For some reason, he and my mother were married and later separated after my birth. Shortly afterward, he moved to Boston with his other siblings to find work. He had only a third- or fourth-grade education, and fundamental reading and writing was a challenge for him. He worked as a butcher in a meat market while in Georgia. Whenever he would visit us from Boston, I remember him always smelling of alcohol. This is less than a perfect picture of what a little girl expects of a dad. My mother shared no information about what caused the breakdown in their relationship. So I was left to formulate my own opinion, and the devil was right there to assist me in this task. So as a child, I decided to excel academically. If I was smart enough, then he would be proud of me and would want to be a part of my life. I set out on this journey of academic excellence and succeeded, but my dad was still not around. What could I do to make him love me? What could I do to make him pay attention to me? I was smart and cute (or so I thought), and who wouldn't want to be a part of my life?

I grew up with this misconception of not being loved and unwanted. I wanted the love of a father. I sought this in guys. I gained their attention, but it never went beyond that point. I was not promiscuous but longed for love. You might say that I was a tease, and I'm perfectly okay with that term.

Years would go by, and I would not even get a call from my dad. His phone number would change often, and if you could reach him, the phone would be disconnected. I lived with the void in my life for many years. After graduating from college, I was introduced to this guy on a blind date, and his name was Ezell. Ezell played college football and certainly looked the part. He was different. He was a gentle giant, and we connected immediately. He read the encyclopedia for fun. He was kind yet quirky but very smart. On our first date, we ate at Wendy's and later went back to my apartment and watched episodes of *Andy Griffith*. We talked for hours. We met when he was enrolled in college at Southern Illinois University and was home on summer break. We dated for four years in a long-distance relationship. We married in 1992. He was perfect for me. My brother walked me down the aisle and gave me away in marriage. At that time, I didn't even know where my dad was living or how to reach him, so at least he could attend the nuptials. To me, this is the ultimate rejection and abandonment.

I learned as I got older that my father had gotten involved in drugs, and his mental illness had taken a toll on his capacity to make rational decisions. One day, he called me out of the blue. It took me by surprise. He had managed to track me down, which was quite impressive for a man who was basically illiterate. We reconnected, and I had been married for quite some time and had given birth to twin girls whom he had never met. He called to tell me that he was hearing voices again. This was a normal conversation for me now. Whenever we talked, it seemed so awkward. I obliged him and asked him what the voices were saying to him this time. He said this voice was different. He said the voice told him that he was going to die soon. My dad said that it startled him because no one was in the room and that the TV was turned off. Who was speaking to him? I believe it was the voice of God that he was hearing, and it was a warning to get his life in order. He was sixty-five years old when we had this conversation. My dad began smoking cigarettes when he was around thirteen years old. At this point, he had smoked for about fifty years and had developed emphysema. Nothing would stop him from smoking. Once I received a call from him, and he was in the hospital. He was afraid but wouldn't tell me so, but I knew it. I was able to walk him through the prayer of salvation. After being dismissed from the hospital, he continued his rambunctious lifestyle. He connected with and began dating a woman who was also mentally ill. This relationship was volatile. She would call at 2:00 a.m. and ask me to referee their frequent fights. At this point, my dad respected me and would do anything that I asked. I became the parent, and now he was the child. The conversations would end with him saying, "I'll do whatever you say, baby girl." My relationship with my dad during my formulative years was nonexistent. However, we developed some type of relationship as I became an adult. It wasn't ideal, but it was mine. I knew he loved me in his own special way because he respected me as his daughter.

With rejection and abandonment also came shame. I was ashamed of my dad. I remember going on a family vacation to Maine. We drove to Boston so that my kids could finally meet their grandfather. They were around thirteen years old at the time. When we arrived, my dad opened the door in his underwear and asked me to come inside. I asked my kids and my husband to step away from the door. I explained to my dad that he had guests and he needed to get dressed. He said okay and proceeded to put on his pants. Mental illness is real. He invited us into his apartment, and the living conditions were deplorable. There was trash all over the floor. We sat and talked to him for a while, and I took him to buy groceries. After this visit, I knew then that I would never allow my kids to witness this tragedy. I still apologize for this event. I was so ashamed, and I went back to my hotel and cried from the embarrassment that I had just witnessed. My children were a little more understanding. They kept reassuring me that it was okay, but I wasn't okay. I had shared with my cousin that I was coming to Boston and to let my dad know because his phone was disconnected again. She assured me that she would relay the message. Why wasn't he prepared for our visit?

I was ashamed of his mental illness, and I was ashamed of the drug use. I became angry because I wanted him to be normal, but he wasn't. Why couldn't I have been born to normal parents? I remember how my dad would make promises that he would never keep. I remember one promise in particular. He had said that he would buy me a pink bicycle for Christmas. Well, when Christmas came, there was no pink bicycle. My birthday was in January, and he promised that I would definitely get the bicycle for my birthday. However, another broken promise. This plagued me for many years. I became very angry with my dad. We have a picture in our mind of what we want our parents to look like, sound like, and treat us in a certain way. When things don't happen the way that we think they should, we become frustrated and angry. I know I was. Anger comes from setting unrealistic expectations that we place on another individual. The Bible says that in Acts 8, Paul was killing Christians because they were believers. At this time, he was an unbeliever. Because people were different from him, he was angry and chose to kill them. This is manipulation and control in its highest form. When we take the limitations off of people and accept them right where they are, we release freedom to them and ourselves. We can't make people be something that they are not. This is the job of the Holy Spirit. Ask God to change the way that you feel toward that person and love them right where they are. This allows us to obtain freedom from anger and expectations. This is what Christ did for us. He loved us in our own sin and accepted us as His beloved according to Ephesians 1:6. No matter who or what he was, he was still my dad—mental illness, drug addiction, and all. I didn't like it, but I chose to accept him.

Journey to Restoration and Healing

Before all of these events had transpired with my dad, I had grown in my relationship with my heavenly Father. I had learned to forgive my dad for not being a part of my life. I asked God to heal *all* my wounds that had been created because of this rejection and abandonment that had been birthed in my heart as a child. God is so faithful. He healed me, and I was able to take care of my dad while living in New Orleans and he lived in Boston. The trips were expensive, but that was my job. I can freely talk to people about my own experiences and not feel the pain anymore because *I am healed*! Healing is not just for cancer patients but for the brokenhearted. God said in Luke 4:18 (KJV) that He came to heal the brokenhearted. I was no longer bitter, but I was forgiven. I released forgiveness toward him, and I received forgiveness from my heavenly Father.

As I grew in my knowledge of the Lord, I also learned about generational curses. I began to identify with the fact that perhaps my grandfather was not a good parent to my dad. Maybe my dad learned about rejection from him. I don't know the answer to this to be true, but I do know that my dad could not give me what he had not received himself. Children learn by example. Maybe he had not received love and acceptance from his father and didn't know how to give it to me. I believe that he wanted to be a good dad but didn't know how. This is how I learned that this spirit of rejection would not be imputed into my DNA and to my generational line. With this ammunition of knowledge in my pocket, I became less angry with my dad for his behavior. I was determined that I would be different. Because I didn't receive the love and acceptance that I fully needed, I chose to saturate my children in love. I would and still do tell them how much I love and appreciate them. I hug them, kiss them, and spend quality time with them. I even leave love notes in the bathroom or in their room. The love overflows in my house until they ask me to leave them alone. One thing is certain: they know that they are loved.

My dad died on December 19, 2014, from a drug overdose and alcohol intoxication. He was seventy-nine years old. I couldn't change who he was, but I changed the way I felt toward him. I asked God to help me to see him as Christ saw him. My whole perspective changed. I became more patient with him during his remaining time on earth. There is no way that I could've done this except God equipped me. My husband was a huge support in helping me to get to a better place with my relationship with my dad.

My journey with my dad was not easy. It allowed me to change who I was.

I hope that my story will encourage and strengthen you to get to a better place in your own spiritual journey and relationship with a family member or loved one. There are so many opportunities to hold grudges and walk in unforgiveness. However, this is not the plan that God designed for your life. "Then said He unto His disciples, 'It is impossible but that offenses will come, but woe unto him through whom they come'" (Luke 17:1, KJV).

It is important that we find a plan to address the offenses that crop up in our lives. We have to find a place of forgiveness. This is a commandment that God requires of each of us. "And when you stand praying, forgive, if you have ought against anyone; so that your Father, who is in heaven, may also forgive you your transgressions" (Mark 11:25, KJV).

As you have read my story, I hope that the Holy Spirit has brought some people or certain situations to your mind that you need to address. If this is the case, I want to take you through a prayer of forgiveness. Please read the prayer below out loud and put anyone's name in the space provided. You may not feel any different, but it's important to make the confession. "If we confess our sins, he is faithful and just to forgive us our sins, and to cleanse us from all unrighteousness" (1 John 1:9, KJV).

Dear Heavenly Father,

I chose to forgive my _____ (mother/father) for rejecting me and abandoning me when I needed him/her the most. I chose to accept You as my heavenly father/mother. Please fill in all the voids that were created by my earthly mother/father. I choose to release all hurt, anger, bitterness from my past. I receive love, joy, acceptance, peace, and healing. I ask that You take Your blood that was shed on the cross and apply it to this wound that was created by my mother/father. I release forgiveness toward them, and I receive Your forgiveness. I ask that You heal every wound, and I apply Your dunamis resurrection power to this wound. I decree and declare that I am no longer held captive by these deadly emotions. I am set free in Jesus's name! (Repeat three times.)

    I repeated this prayer over and over again. I didn't feel any different, but I knew that God was transforming my heart. Romans 10:17 says that faith comes by hearing and hearing by the Word of God. I had to hear myself say this whether I believed it in my heart. Faith is not a feeling. The more I confessed this prayer, my anger became less and less.

    Anger is an emotion. Emotions are real and need to be healed as well. Even though my dad was no longer here on the earth, there were emotions that I needed to address. My dad would make promises to me that he never kept. I remember being angry and disappointed about those broken promises. I didn't believe anything that he said. My believer was broken and wasn't operating properly. This had to be repaired. When I first got saved, I associated my earthly father with my heavenly Father. This is a wrong perception to have about the Creator of the universe. There were promises in the God's holy Word that are true. However, "God is not a man, that he should lie; neither the son of man, that he should repent: hath he said, and shall he not do it? Or hath he spoken, and shall he not make it good" (Numbers 23:19, KJV)?

    I had held so many feelings in my heart for so many years, and now was the time to surrender every bit of it to Jesus. My heart was being transformed. God was chipping away at the broken pieces of my heart. The Spirit of the Lord is upon me because

> The Lord hath anointed me to preach good tidings unto the meek; he hath sent me to bind up the brokenhearted, to proclaim liberty to the captives, and the opening of the prison to them that are bound to comfort all that

mourn; To appoint unto them that mourn in Zion, to give unto them beauty for ashes, the oil of joy for mourning, the garment of praise for the spirit of heaviness; that they might be called trees of righteousness, the planting of the Lord, that he might be glorified. (Isaiah 61:1–3, KJV)

I was able to forgive my dad for all the things that held me captive for such a long time. My heart was healed. I want you to experience the same freedom that I encountered. Jesus died to set us free. He came to set us free from past hurts. He is concerned about everything that concerns us. I am able to walk in the same freedom that Jesus died to give us. My story may not be your story, but pain feels the same. A broken heart looks and feels the same in everyone.

I look at the relationship that my husband has with our daughters, and I am thankful that God has given them a loving father. He's not perfect, but they are able to feel the love of a father in a way that I never knew. They have a relationship with their dad that makes them view their heavenly Father in a different way. I pray that this book has helped you in some way. I trust that you are on your journey to restoration and healing. Don't allow the enemy to steal the true revelation of God's word by holding onto unforgiveness. Repent today and start to experience the abundant life that Christ died to give us.

About the Author

Carla and her husband, Ezell reside in New Orleans, Louisiana with their twins, Lindsey and Christa Shelton. They attend City Church of New Orleans. Carla and Ezell hold weekly Bible study lessons in their home. They partner together in helping others to grow in the knowledge and love of Jesus Christ. Carla has a practical way of sharing the word of God so that others can relate and their lives be transformed. It is her desire that people walk in forgiveness and the freedom that Jesus died for us to have. When we release forgiveness, we are set free and the thief can no longer rob us of our destiny.

CPSIA information can be obtained
at www.ICGtesting.com
Printed in the USA
LVHW091559300421
686095LV00020B/338